Hi, my name is Penny! A weird thing has been happening in my city, lately.

My sister says that she feels like our lives have been turned upside down.
I feel that way, too.

Everything is different than it used to be.
We're all staying home a lot more.

I haven't been to school in a while.
I do all of my school work from a desk in my house.

My brothers and I can't go to the playground to play with our friends anymore.

Sometimes all of the changes make me feel sad.
My mom told me it is okay to feel sad.

I asked her "why does our life feel like it was turned upside down? Why is everything different now?"
She said that what we are experiencing is called a *pandemic*.
I had never heard the word pandemic before.
It sounded scary.

My dad explained to me that a pandemic is something that people around the WORLD
experience at the same time.
Like, how a lot of people are feeling sick right now with covid-19.

"So, everyone's lives are upside down, all around the world?" I asked.
"Yes, sweetheart," he replied. "Upside down, all around. We are all in this together."
That really made me think. Wow! All around the world!

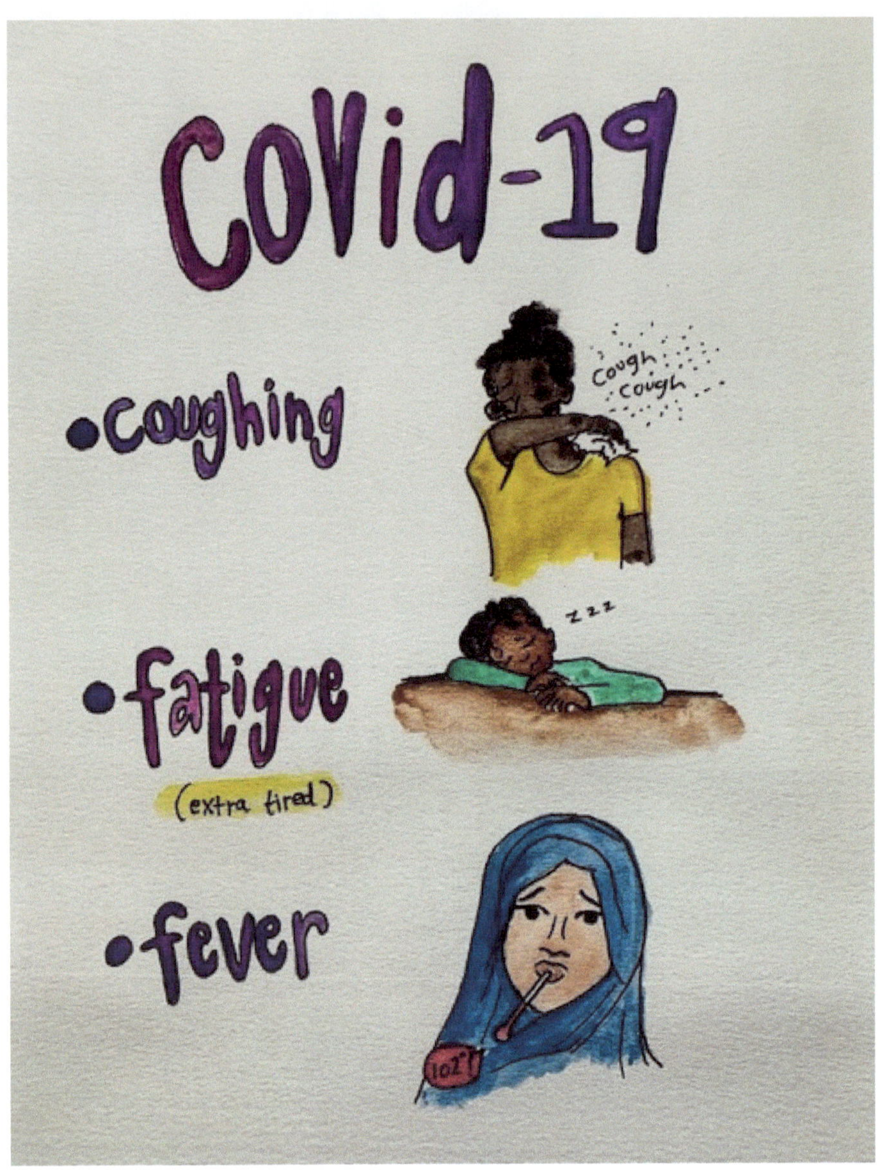


"But, what is covid-19?" I asked my mom.
"It's a new illness caused by a virus that can spread from person to person," my mother explained.
She told me it can make us cough and feel very tired.
It can make our foreheads hot from a fever.

She also told me about the doctors and nurses and scientists and first responders who are
working very hard to keep us safe and to help us turn our lives right side up, again.
But, it will take some time.

It made me feel happy to know that so many people are helping!
My dad told me that there are things we can do to help keep the whole world safer, too!

We can wash our hands extra times a day, with soap and water, while counting to 20 or singing the ABCs.

We can practice social distance. I wasn't sure what social distance meant, but my dad explained to me that it means staying 6 feet or more away from people who do not live in our house.

So, it's okay to run through the sprinklers with my little brother!

Or to teach the baby how to ride his tricycle.

Or to have a fun cookout in my backyard with my family.

But, if my friends want to say hi, they need to stay on the sidewalk. I can wave at them from my house and we can tell each other funny jokes!

When we go out in public to get things we need, we can wear a face mask that covers our mouth and nose and we can put gloves on our hands.

We can wash our clothes when we get home. This helps protects us from any icky germs.

It's very important to clean things that we touch a lot.
Like, doorknobs and counter tops!

Some days will still feel upside down.

But, now I know how I can do my part to help keep myself, my friends and my family safe all around!

WASHING HANDS
SOCIAL DISTANCE
6 feet apart
clean Surfaces
MASKS & GLOVES

It feels good to know that we are all in this together.
We will get through it together, too.

*Dedicated to my children. My tiny superheroes.*